CHIEMI

ODD

SIMPLE

Beauty

For more information about Chiemi, go to
www.ChiemiMusic.com

Table of Contents

1. Chasing Light With Darkness

We're still emerging from the darkness of quarantine and isolation. Hopefully, we can move into the light without forgetting the parts of the experience of darkness that make it now so much brighter. Darkness gives light contour, so much more depth than we realize. Recognizing that is what these are about.

1. Never Exactly Here Again
2. Things You Don't Expect
3. Much More Than Shelter
4. Airspace
5. Leaves in Life
6. Well of Wonder
7. Sequential Selves
8. Tracking Goblins
9. Always Time to Climb
10. Mental Missives

PHOTO BY ARI GOODMAN

PHOTO BY ARI GOODMAN

Never Exactly Here Again ∽ 9/30/21, 10/1/21,

We want to chase the light, yet retain the darkness,
The dark that brings light, so much depth
That it's brighter now, than before,
Brings new dimensions, opens doors.

When you've been through fire, you come out with less innocence,
And a love of life, a knowing one, each moment at once,
Pleasure heightened by the thought,
That we'll never be here again.

We want to measure time, in a way that's poetic,
Feeling this strange energy that's chaotic,
Flickering from below, stitching back
To our melodic overflow.

With hands on my knees, notes spilling out on the floor,
There's a stillness and power, vitality and what it means,
For survival to soar.

We want to re-mix music, with the reality,
That there's always a noxious side,
That we're mortal, can't save the world,
Must submit to greater forces, turmoil.

PHOTO BY KIRA SEAMON

Birds on sand, together and apart,
A dolphin's tail past the reef.
To retrieve pieces of the past,
Our songs are charged and brief.

Desert and water, an iceberg tip,
To retain them's like trying to catch light.
But a melody, we'll recall,
Adheres to our inner sight.

Where we were, how we felt,
Tunes wind inside our heads.
Notes answering or asking questions,
Magic present when they're things you don't expect.

We keep contradictory truths,
Iconic, ironic, real and fake.
Those that change and fall apart,
Mind bending moments for their own sake.

Life's inherent cadence, seeps in like milestone memories –
Your childhood home, a concert with a friend, the scent of candy from a
factory.
They're shapes within shapes, eyes and ears changing focus,
Moving them through the world, part of your locus.

We yearn for transformative times,
Healing words swerving into lushness.
For universe, sound, and nature,
To converge, as sustenance.

PHOTO BY ARI GOODMAN

Much More Than Shelter

There's a path to the house,
Through the sticks of all sticks,
Woods surrounding and enlivening, a rare chance for solace,
With a rush of freedom.

Technological noise, cannot penetrate there,
So you must open your eyes,
Glimpse water, a dividing wall,
Stone like an accordion.

Human habitat's much more than shelter.
It's happiness in space fulfilled,
Emotional equilibrium in a chosen place,
Belongings left where those held close can stay. Can stay.

Dematerialization aesthetic,
Creates a pleasant uncertainty.
Where does the building stand?
Home an outgrowth of the land?

Sorrow can render experience large and strange,
But can also help us find, our common story,
Tears landing like jazz chords, on resonating memories.

It's hallucinogenic realism,
And who or what it possesses,
The pressure that grief,
Exerts on expression.

PHOTO BY WERNER SCHROFFNER

Airspace ⤳

There's an airspace laced, with placid coral strokes,
Palm frond silhouettes, buildings like lavender pegs,
In the shadows of the city below.

Gilt-edged, fading warmth, slips beneath the horizon,
By darkened trees along the ridges,
Water serene and surrounding.

When you're left to do what you can't avoid,
You do what's helpless and vital,
Lose the distance between thinking and saying,
Connect what's viable and can't be set aside.

The luminous view from the top of a roof, imparts a bewildering sense,
Of being in touch with things bigger than yourself,
Where everything and nothing is fixed.

If a new tale can transpire, perhaps we require, a different language,
One not fraught with cliché and anger.
If a new tune's made, to carry the day, maybe it can be wrought,
From sounds that convey, a better sense of play.

Re-natured prose, words like petals,
Open portals to another kind of world alongside us,
Visible, invisible and understood.

PHOTO BY ARI GOODMAN

Leaves in Life ~~~

So many leaves, bright in the light,
Falling, turning, disintegrating.
We catch them, save them, let them go,
While their birthing tree remains.

Something can be a miracle, and a trick all at once,
But changing your life is the ultimate one,
Touring within your transformed self,
Dropping old tools, remembering how you felt.

Things on a slope, must keep their balance,
Watching, sensing, adjusting.
We move, we dance, hold each other,
Even a tree has roots underground.

When things happen, who knows what's good or bad?
We only know that they did, and whether we're happy or sad.
Feelings inspire empathy, open us to something else,
Survivors until others survive us.

Rituals should help us break patterns,
Musing, testing, trying as we may,
We connect, reflect, become different people,
Letting life improvise, the music we play.

PHOTO BY KATRINA WINZELER

Well of Wonder ᘒ

Shadows beckon, black fully chromatic,
Melodies confounding, and natural.
Though it raises you up, love also sustains,
Lights you from inside, on empty days,
A well from which to engage.

Soft ripples on water,
Glisten as they still.
A climber nearby, projects its pattern,
Propelling the vision, an intersecting dance.

We take the unvarnished,
Make it familiar, pristine,
Find similar sounds in these spaces,
Deeply, slowly, invite the unseen.

It's like a call to prayer, haunting, sudden, unexpected when it ends.
Like an old poem, in the final act of loving,
Bare, unburdened, full of wonder, again … wonder again …

Striations orange and pink,
Cross the sky, fringed by trees.
Knowledge feeds the stories we see,
Which sets the powers free.

PHOTO BY ARI GOODMAN

Sequential Selves

(You) compare yourself, to yourself, yesterday.
(Or) maybe years ago, when you were here,
As if a window to infinity's been opened.
(You) see your selves, as they are,
In and out of sequence, unbroken.

There's a journey, I am still on it, still going, God willing ...
Leaning against trees, using my body to see,
How things form and recede.

There are places, where beauty's born of gentleness,
That seems to stay the same, while we come back, changed,
Always something to attain.

There's rushing wind, here, tossing the foliage,
Stirring sounds that connect you, to other stories, different selves,
Things that weren't in view.

Travel's in the soul, not just space and time,
And also in dreams, where we absorb what's real and learn what's true,
Where the invisible's revealed, the hidden debuted.

There are movements, here, certain rhythm created,
The stories that emerge when you play, chord and earth vibrations
That line your pathway.

PHOTO BY CHUCK SHEEHAN

Tracking Goblins ～〰 11/24, 26-27/2021

If you sit, long enough you'll see,
Light, carve a life across the sand.
Silhouettes become acquaintances,
Telling time by the shadows that land.

Clouds in this place, of sandstone creatures,
Render them cryptic and wise.
It's a landscape of dulled quietude,
Teeming with glyphs, hermetic sky.

These symphonic forms, enthrall on their own,
Like visual equivalents of sound.
Stages of liberated dance,
Energized strands, geometry bound.

Each one's a whittled moment, like scrimshaw,
But messy, cultivated by wind.
While the beating radiance of the sun,
Rises up, like a living thing.

Goblin figures merge, like liquid stone, static and changeable as bone.
What's visible conveys, a parallel premise, together while apart's got
benefits.

It's an atmosphere where everything mixes,
Without melting into one.
A paradigm of vital immersion,
Where identities aren't undone.

PHOTO BY ARI GOODMAN

Always Time to Climb

Stillness can be your best weapon.
For permitting yourself,
To experience rather than produce.
To engage, rather than control.

When the sun's in your eyes,
And you'd rather fly,
Enjoy the view on the way.
'Cause there's always time to climb … always time to climb.

When you're still, you can channel,
The ineffable, the intangible
Strings of experience, into something good,
Auditory and shared.

Tranquility and notes, can prompt introspection,
Conjure feelings, with or without words.
Music can be, a higher revelation,
Than all wisdom and philosophy.

Regardless of whether you're productive,
Life is happening,
Unveiling passing sparkles,
Wonder born, of odd simple beauty.

PAINTING BY LEAH SALOW

SOMETIMES PLACES PEOPLE LOVE CAN EVOKE THEM. MY FATHER-IN-LAW, WHO PASSED AWAY IN THE FALL OF 2021, ADORED MT. DESERT ISLAND, WHICH THIS PAINTING DEPICTS A PART OF.

Mental Missives

Grief's an emotion so large
It has no edges.
Roles we think won't be us,
Balancing on ledges.

To send a letter's to
Believe it will be read,
Not a time and place,
When someone's dead.

But mental missives come
When you're in a spot loved by someone.
You feel the person there,
In the seaweed, rocks and air.

You can make writing
A form of dialogue,
The intimate texture of conversation,
With no memory to jog.

Remembering makes the world vibrate with humor, wit and tenderness,
Feelings recognized in others, 'cause we're not so different ... not so
different.

It's a lovely fantasy,
Turned into a shared reality
With others reminiscing,
Messages sent out with the sea.

II. Finding Space in Brightness

We seek the light and are sometimes blinded by it. Stunned. But when you close your eyes, you can still feel the warmth, see the glowing golden tint behind your lids – your own space in the brightness. These songs are about that.

11. Not Blinded
12. Built From Time
13. Barefoot View
14. Sunlight
15. When We Begin
16. Swan Sentiments
17. All That's Left is Zen
18. Woods and Faces
19. Haven Space
20. Illusionary Grace

PHOTO BY ARI GOODMAN

PHOTO BY ARI GOODMAN

Not Blinded ⌒⌒

There are moments when we wish
We could stop time or slow it down,
Faced with something so divine and deeply joyful,
We wish it were prolonged … prolonged.

We seek the light, and can get blinded.
But when you close your eyes,
You feel the warmth, primed.

When you close your eyes, there's a glowing tint,
Your space in the brightness,
Safe behind your lids.

We seek inspiration, without burning in a flash,
How to stretch the present minute,
Save it from slipping into the past.

Recovery's about personal discovery.
Behind the boundaries of a comfortable reality,
Being transformed by imagining with clarity,
Being transformed to really see … really see.

We seek to turn, the moment into a lifetime,
Because what you love, seizes your passion,
Affects everything.

PAINTING BY LEAH SALOW

Built From Time ～ 12/17/2021 & 1/3-4/2022

You feel the intensity,
Painting the water and sky.
No boredom in the silence,
Just a feeling of being alive.

Notes of shade and luster,
A monstrous, angled blaze.
Caught in time, like all of us,
Just a moment on the stage.

Time's the fourth dimension,
What makes a square a cube.
How we travel to the future,
Based on what we choose … based on what we choose.

Do we turn from a sunset?
Look away to the trees?
As much as we are pushed by the past,
Hope affects what we see.

Time can be a building block, and also a measuring stick,
And the substance of everything in existence.
Time travels through us, as we travel through it –
We're built from time, bit by bit …

What's terrifying about time,
Is part of its design.
While our bodies reside in the present,
Our past reveals the sublime.

PHOTO BY ARI GOODMAN

Barefoot View ∼⌐

You want to take a barefoot view,
Step into the scenery,
Exercise absence of logic,
Slip away through the greenery.

The appeal of unrequited love,
Saves you from the act.
There's no real threat of failure,
Keeps the glamour intact.

It's impossible, infinitely irresistible,
Emanating silliness and love.
Sending out notes in the air, creates an atmosphere,
What dreams are made of.

Do you want to chase a mirage,
That won't give the promise it held?
Better leave it, intricately balanced,
Floating with, surprises where we dwell.

Don't be afraid of dark places, patchy scattered shapes and spaces.
If you can find a light to shine, treasures revealed might be divine.
Surfaces have an intimacy, begging to be touched.
If you can reach them with your hand, things that are hidden say much.

We all have our own deserts,
Where the sands are not the same,
That we're compelled to cross,
Nor forgetting from whence we came.

PHOTO BY KATRINA WINZELER

Sunlight ⌒⌒

Some things we don't see, until there's sunlight,
Or some mysterious agency, brings form to sight.
Nonetheless, they are there,
Coming to life in the glare … in the glare.

Gold flickers against blackness,
And we've left the city,
It's labyrinthine alleys and secrecy,
In rearview mirrors of what's to be.

Now there's light in the kitchen,
Weak and geometric,
Landscape ablaze, a photo to take,
The illusion of control and transcendence.

Precarious peace can be shattered in an instant.
Tragedy can lurk and bleed,
Hurtful words said or screamed.
But weaponized middle age can pause and see.

It's an age when we don't have to be wise, but know, at least, what's ill
advised.

When we're stubborn enough to stay the course, too vain or practical to
feel remorse.
When you pause and see, those words can just be,
Sounds taking them, somewhere free… where love is always the key.
The connections that bind us,
Are astounding and invisible,
Pulling in places we can't see or feel,
That only, make sense in time, when they're real.

PHOTO BY ARI GOODMAN

When We Begin 〜⌒   1/18-20/2022

It's impossible to hide from yourself.
The sound's already in your ear.
The hardest part is listening,
And it's possible to find yourself, anywhere … anywhere.

You, the camera and subject,
All become one in an image.
If you're adored from behind the lens,
The viewer can sense the tenderness.

How do we look at a rainbow?
Or waves much greater than anyone?
We're tangible beings and revel in that,
Capturing moments to retain when we're done.

So we try to create things,
That will outlive the experience,
Exist without us, out of time,
Pictures and stories for others to find.

Invisible connections, exist that can be read, messages sent by the living
and the dead.
Art can be a vessel, for use as a mirror, entryway to the past, who we are
and what might last.

And how to tell it, so
It's not just a shared delusion?
As once said by Didion,
We know how to write when we begin.

PHOTO BY KIRA SEAMON

Swan Sentiments ⟿

Swans send their calls, over the water,
Like sunlight shining on gold,
Instruments roused, seeing in color,
Maintaining expressions, shy and bold.

Sometimes you're awakened,
Hear sounds, feel recognized,
Notes greeting, something inside you,
That no one else can see, now alive.

Cygnets understand, the power of chance,
The smallest decisions have significance.
Whether to fly low or immerse to catch a fish,
What you see under water may be different.

They're babies born grey, brown before they're white,
In real time, learning their senses,
We can but observe, their watchful eyes,
Imagining what's seen, from behind their lenses.

How do we carry, the experience of change, transitioning, beginning and
ending?
Like developing swans, we often shift direction, stop abruptly, switch our
feathers,
On our way to becoming something else, altogether.

Process influences results, in so many ways,
Sky versus the pond's ultramarine,
Looking from above, or diving below,
Humans, grass and gravel, seen or unseen.

HOTO BY ARI GOODMAN

All That's Left is Zen

You can enter a garden,
Walk around, leave it behind.
Or it can enter you,
So you're as tranquil as what you find.

You hope to carry some
Of the stillness away with you,
The space between absence
And presence, to carry through.

We need to go beyond ourselves.
The world won't shrink to our size.
Expand to meet it, for life's outside.
Go towards it, where it resides.

Experience is less important
Than what you make of it.
Lemon globes in lush branches,
Violets in a corner, where a butterfly's lit.

Aesthetic can be less about accumulation than subtraction.
Whatever remains is everything.
Contemplation can be less about analysis than being.
Embracing the whole gives you wings.

Colors bleed in and out,
Reflecting things around them.
Rose petals catching light,
And all that's left is zen.

SCULPTURES BY ERIC KAIN HUMPHREYS

Woods and Faces ～◦

Woods and faces, images and crevices,
What's to see, not to see.
Prolonged turmoil, in an expression.
Eye sockets cast a dark sheen.

It's something hard to speak about,
The state it can put you into,
And why this knocked you down so hard,
Pierced you through.

Maybe it's to do with the time when it happened,
And that you so clearly saw,
An alternate future mapping,
And that's not what happened at all.

Do we have statues in effigy, in our minds waiting to be resolved?
Their simple being's just a memory, not a spirit on which to call.
Not all puzzles need to be solved.

The way some things hit us,
Can be surprising and weird.
Days ticking away,
Losing someone, more or less severe.

PHOTO BY ARI GOODMAN

Haven Space 〜⌒

Some people, the more they show themselves,
The less you can say who they really are.
When a rainbow blends into the sky,
Is it still the sum of its parts?

It's that element in creativity,
A tradition in contradiction,
Which does not change at its core,
Just constantly, in its expression.

Some journeys, the more they go on,
The less you can say where they're going.
A road, when it comes to an end,
Can lead to where another path's showing.

Playing a part's deep down, about seeing yourself in a much larger whole,
That if you can play your part perfectly, can be a greater sum total.
Playing a part's also, about finding a chosen place,
Where, if it's safe to grow, can be both a haven and open space.

Some music, when it ends,
You continue to hear, again and again,
Echoing in the rooms of your heart,
Calling you to wake and start.

KATRINA AND I PERFORMED THIS TUNE BY HER A FEW TIMES IN 2005, AND IT WAS NICE TO BE ABLE TO RECREATE THE EXPERIENCE A LITTLE, SO MANY YEARS LATER, WITH THIS RECENT MIX OF RECORDED LEAD VOCALS, GUITAR AND HARMONY TRACKS (HTTPS://SOUNDCLOUD. COM/USER-377401109/ILLUSIONARY-GRACE AND HTTPS://CHIEMI1. BANDCAMP.COM/TRACK/ILLUSIONARY-GRACE-FEAT-KATRINA-WINZELER), AS WELL AS SO MUCH FUN TO INCLUDE IT IN THIS BOOK.

Illusionary Grace ✐

3/19/22 originally 2005
by Katrina Winzeler

Last Monday, I stood against a concrete wall, and looked up at the sky,
And it, it looked back down at me, and it, it pulled to me a fire that I
hadn't seen in years
I simply wither if I can't have you. If I can't have … you.

The tassels on my purple sweater were flames of desire I cast behind my
eyes
My eyes overlooked them and I, as hard as I seem
I've got one foot in reality, and the other one is in a dream.

And I know it's illusionary grace, that brings me back to life, I can't stop
thinking of your face.
You're like a mystery, forever out of sight. Yeah, and, just singing songs
tonight. I am singing songs in the night.

I saw you yesterday, and I nearly lost my breath.
You're like a phantom dancing through my fantasies, and I want so badly
to melt into your eyes,
But this earth is too cruel and I sleep alone at night. I sleep alone at
night.

I lay weeping, listening to music, I could have anyone. I am only want-
ing you
And the absurdity does nothing to deter me from this dream,
I am invaded by a package, and that's not like what it seems.

Please don't ask me to be strong in this. I feel such loss should be so
evident.
You're like a taste of something scattered in the light, yeah, and just sing-
ing songs tonight.

And I know it's illusionary grace, that brings me back to life, I can't stop thinking of your face.

You're like a mystery, forever out of sight. Yeah, and just singing songs tonight.

iii. A Place to Grow:
Charting the Swoon

We're coming back, despite lingering vestiges of the pandemic. But back to where? Home has changed shape, but at the very least, we hope it's safe, a place to collect ourselves, regenerate, and grow.

Separately, a friend heard "Charting the Swoon," said it reminded him of selections from Godspell (which he loves☺), and suggested that it should be a title track, so I've incorporated it into what this group of songs are called.

1. What You're Dreaming On
2. Trip From the Void
3. No Token
4. Common Means
5. What's Told
6. Frozen Scene
7. A Thousand Facets
8. Pummel
9. Charting the Swoon
10. From a Distance

PHOTO BY ARI GOODMAN

PHOTO BY ARI GOODMAN

What You're Dreaming On

What's growth that you can see,
From the perspective of a balcony?
It's not as simple as green palms,
Just something to be found.

When you breath in you're more attuned,
To the world where you'll resume,
Approaching the unfamiliar with curiosity,
And not intractability.

There's infinite power in a pause,
Gathering silence in an embrace.
Acknowledging the present moment,
Allowing our selves to show up in space.

You can't tell someone to find,
The questions and passions that'll shape their lives.
But you can expose them to things,
Wonder that an experience can bring.

We see it happen all the time.
People volunteer at a shelter, or travel in a profound way.
Beginning to ask what part they can play.
With any luck, that's how it starts. And with a pause it can go far.

When you have time to reflect,
On your response in every aspect.
In that place lies growth and freedom,
For a new one that you're dreaming on.

PHOTO BY WERNER SCHROFFNER

Trip From the Void ✑

Imagine yourself, unspooling into a void.
Light returns, breaking the spell,
Landing you heavily and lightly, all at once,
Hollowed out tones, ringing inside like a bell.

Sometimes something happens,
And there's no way to be, the person you were before.
There's a little freedom in every loss, no matter how unlooked for.
Like reincarnation, one life ends, and another's got an open door.

The darkness of a protracted crisis
Can be all-consuming, forcing a choice,
Lean in or look away,
Embrace nihilism or try to find joy.

When you enter a cave, you can turn on a lantern,
Chilled air, with a pomelo glow.
You see a flicker, perhaps a phantom,
In your head, fear of a ledge that's faux.

What looks like paradise, can be a diaphanous curtain,
behind which lies decay.
In ever changing times, goals can shift and sway.

Leaving a cave, you feel the brightness.
Brutal directness, like an allegory.
We all want a homecoming,
But its definition's not yet part of the story.

PHOTO BY ARI GOODMAN

No Token

A little off, a little unloved,
Maybe a little haunted.
Nothing actually keeps danger
From being dangerous.

You take that energy,
Move with a different sheen,
Seek new spells, transformative power,
Misfits feel like they're seen.

It's not safety that keeps us from being afraid.
It's love ... that keeps fear at bay.
So we can experience the undivided
Gift of being alive. Alive.

Confident peculiarities point towards pluralism,
Vibrant minds and hearts
In between split acculturation.
Without apology, speaking's a start.

We don't want to be a token ornament to naïve idealism.
In belonging there's warmth, but there can also be realism.
Faith doesn't guarantee your well-being,
But you can live yourself into a new way of seeing.

This doesn't elide cultural boundaries,
But rather their surefire potency.
It electrifies their aesthetic flair
And emotional buoyancy.

PAINTING BY LEAH SALOW

Common Means

A cabin on a dock's
A shelter for boats
To be collected and kept,
A common means to be off.

We don't learn how to love through will power,
But experience of being,
Bonds forged from everyday things that we share,
A way of living, not just a feeling. Not just a feeling.

There's a visual tension,
Light not coming from above,
But shimmering on the mist through the trees,
As if from another dimension.

The sea's like a graveyard,
Where worlds were swallowed up,
Waiting to be re-discovered,
Like optical illusions on a card.

The opposite of envy is celebration.
When we live for the good of others, there's elation.
Love follows and surrounds us, in ways we don't realize,
Invisible threads that strengthen and surprise.

It's mainstream and esoteric.
There's no aesthetic hierarchy.
All things in nature are connected.
It's not a meritocracy.

PHOTO BY ARI GOODMAN

What's Told ⌇⌇⌇   3/8-11/2022

There's no real end point, where music's been learned.
It's always a pursuit of more.
Further understanding, broadening ability, ideas to explore.

With a different instrument, there are crisp edges,
Diagonal movement, liberating sounds it dredges.

A view's surface sizzles, sweats and droops in the weather.
Bright palms, slightly acidic, in cake frosting sky like feathers.

There's something about the back and forth, tones that respond.
Feel of the strings, informs direction and thought.

Perhaps there's a flaw, more wood, less metal that's staid.
We can relate to flaws. They might be perfect for the song you want to
play.

Fresh sounds can affect your sight, novel notes changing the spectrum,
Adding to the catalog, altering the tension.
At face value, playing music may not seem essential.
Yet, it can filter, make sense of the world, in a way that feels central.

Musicians are never done.
They play and continue onward.
The new doesn't diminish the old,
Just expands the art of what's told.

PAINTING BY ANDREW BOTTI

Frozen Scene

3/16-17/2022

Branches frosted with winter, in silhouette,
Tinted yellow from the light.
Iridescence lies green on the snow,
Trees with chilled arms, glistening white.

It's something you see in a fairytale,
Still based on what's real,
Crystals in bark, stretched on the shore,
Not what you see, but how it makes you feel.

To grow intellectually, you need to be surprised.
If we're not surprised, we're not learning,
Data, without understanding,
No yeast for our thoughts to rise.

You can move to places until they're familiar,
With different approaches to life.
But can they all be considered home,
Places where you live and thrive?

Do you want an environment that forces you to grow,
Full of daily surprises, whether you seek them out or not?
It can be uncomfortable.
You can also avoid what's new - at least you won't miss what wasn't
sought.

To keep on learning and growing,
Requires avoiding routine,
Like a sunset that bleeds into the sky,
Sets fire to our minds in a frozen scene.

THIS INNSBRUCK PHOTO FROM WHEN I SPENT THE SUMMER OF 1990 IN AUSTRIA WITH RELATIVES AND DID SOME BUSKING IN A COUPLE OF THE PUBLIC GARDENS WHILE I WAS THERE, CAME TO MIND FOR THIS SONG.

A Thousand Facets ~~~

The mind's a place where we are at times at peace,
And sometimes at odds.
A space we inhabit but don't control,
From which there is no pause.

At the center, there's a spot,
Where what's real about us resides,
That we protect from light, although
There's nowhere to go but inside.

And there's a tension between mystery and meaning,
But can you capture experience while hiding its core?
It lies between definition and incoherence,
Something that happens whether you know what it's for.

To protect something significant,
We sometimes flee being known,
While trying to preserve what's paramount,
To preserve it over what's shown.

To get at the unseen essence of what makes us who we are,
We often return to moments precious from afar.
Only to find that we may read them in other ways.
Some things matter more, others have lost their cachet.

We draw the figures of our lives,
In different ways reveal their assets.
At many times, not in one go,
But in a thousand facets.

SCULPTURES BY ERIC KAIN HUMPHREYS

Pummel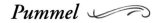

April 2022 - originally 2005

by Katrina Winzeler

It's 4 am, I've got, whiskey in my veins.
Walking home alone, smoking the last of the summer's night.
And they weigh on me like gravity, scout booker to the hype.
The stories of the ones that got away. Pummel me. They pummel me.

Sometimes I catch a memory of your scent upon the breeze.
Cigarettes, laundry to touch and your hair spaced, a name a shiver.
I never felt so close, as I once felt to you.
I still go cold with longing in the deepest part of my being.

Is this, how it's gonna be. You meet someone, have them slip, slip away
in time …
I could never forget you. You'll always be on my mind.
I swear when I take my final breath, I'll still wonder where you are.
Pummels me.

I never got quite over the geometric shape of your lips.
The subtle charm of your undecorated hands.
It was out of my control, on the day I pulled you close.
And now the remains for me are the imprints of your hands.

And I swear, some told love is pain.
Which leave me in hidebound to never … I'll never let myself get hurt again.
I could never forget you… You pummel me …. Oh I really really loved you.

Silhouetted by the moon, you held a bottle of champagne
You were a true work of art, despite your fascist face.
You stuck your hand down my shirt
You said it makes you feel vulnerable …
Like we're back in high school and this was so risqué.   Pummels me.

PHOTO BY ARI GOODMAN

Charting the Swoon ∿‿〜

4/4-5/2022

It's not how much time
You have to work,
But doing it when you work best,
Velvet followed by a fist.

A moment outside
Greets with plumerias,
Birds with their droppings,
The scent of azaleas.

Warp and weft yarns,
Are woven together.
One thread is nothing,
But with others, a treasure.

Human fabrics
Are resilient.
A piece of cloth like a person's life,
Strands and stains of brilliance.

Music's like a utility, belonging to everyone and no one,
Like running water, infusing us with ardor,
Sound bringing a tapestry of words interlaced with wonder. Wonder.

Once you're on the lookout,
You become attuned
To the rhythm of inspiration,
The rise and flow of its swoon.

PHOTO BY KATRINA WINZELER

From a Distance 〜〜

Fear can bring out the awe in us,
Lead us into deeper trust,
Souls engaged in the unknown,
Swapping dread for mystery over what's not shown.

There's an empty white cave,
Filled with ovals of light,
Glimmering on branches with dew,
There will be other moons.

We're together, a community,
Not in our own heads,
But strangers in a shared encounter,
Out of time together.

Does suffering make love more possible?
A moment of wistful clarity,
When we're stranded on an island,
Immaculate sudden parity.

The past is never behind us.
It's hard to say where a past moment ends and an ancestor's time begins,
Something beyond our existence,
Sets the stage for an ending we've only glimpsed from a distance.

Love is a journey,
Following its way through this world,
With a multitude of color,
Rainforest and tree dust.

IV. Reclaiming Our World

It's our world. To reclaim or not. Where do we start? Does it matter? Probably not. And certainly not as much as having that happen at all, in any direction. If that's what we want, and how could we not…

PHOTO BY ANNIKA GOODMAN

Greater Circles ∽

When humanity's in solidarity, with the life cycle.
There's no need for success stories, for ourselves or others.
We're free to be soulful, rather than falsely claiming.

In loving things for themselves, not for what they do for us.
We get ourselves out of the way, take back our world from isolation.
A slow expansion of consciousness, where we're not the reference point.

Waxing and waning, make one curve.
As we love in greater circles, we harmonize our self-care,
With expression beyond ourselves, for our world. For our world.

Moving towards this harmony, concrete and in front of us,
Keeps us from heroic ideals, that are impossible.
Because what we seek, is not just a theory.

When we approach the limit of what human souls can bear,
Empathy can bring us back, so that we care.

The pattern we set, and the tone we take,
Has more weight than any argument, we might make.
History is full of those, whether it's what we emulate.

PHOTO BY KATRINA WINZELER

Earth Fluorescent ⟿ Katrina Winzeler 2005; April 2022

Why do you tell me if I was you, when it's clear that you just don't have a clue.
Of what it's like a summer's gonna do.
I try to wash it off, but it keeps seeping through to me.

Don't think I'm unaware, that I'm the one to blame. Don't think I miss my name in the voice of change.
It's just I am one to believe there's justice in this game. When the comfort I see seeps in bringing me more pain.

Turn earth fluorescent, summer sun. I'm paranoid, starting to need to go home,
These days I drink too much just to have fun. Choking on the same like no one.

So let's sit around and discuss my thoughts on change,
I don't like it. I'd rather sit here forever with my five year rule of your dreams.
It's nice to be away from the city. You should make sure I'll be the child zipper
Where is the pen that I forgot to pack? Showing up without it, doubt I'll be invited back.
The common forces aren't giving out it. I mainly beat on the walls of this chrysalis.
I see your Red Sox, can I hold back my fist? There's gotta be a different kind of life than this.

Turn a, earth fluorescent in the summer sun. I'm paranoid, starting to need to go home,
These days I drink too much just to have fun. Choking on the same like no one.

Cowardly, I thought, at first I'd feel at ease, just believe,
Time to range out how to make you fall in love with me.

Turn a, earth fluorescent, summer sun, I'm paranoid, starting to need to go home,
These days I drink too much just to have fun, I'm choking on the same like no one.
Turn a, earth fluorescent, summer sun,
You turn a, earth fluorescent, in the summer sun,
You turn a, earth fluorescent, in the summer sun,
You turn a, earth fluorescent, in the summer sun.

PHOTO BY ANNIKA GOODMAN

Nature's Exemption

There's nothing that can't be … transfigured.
The whole of creation … waits for it.
Being released into … something else.
Translucent with … grace for it.

Rocks, trees and light, lay bare your very center,
So that it can be changed,
Into something gentle.
The shift is mental.

The feeling of the moment, is channeled onto strings,
Streams of consciousness,
Later transferred to paper,
Remembering their favor.

The first take feels like, communicating something
Beyond comprehension.
Something sublime,
To go back and refine.

Self-donation's a well-spring, opening our lives, to a greater exemption,
Than we could imagine, while mired in possession.

There's self-surrender, and an element of purity.
As if you're a new soul,
Or a child,
Being introduced to life.

PHOTO BY KATRINA WINZELER

Hiding in Color

Are tulips really the place
To keep chicks newly hatched?
I guess the mother should know.
She's watchful while they bask.

Hiding in bright color
Makes you feel alive,
Hues that tint your world
And what you feel inside.

Spring flowers can be someday dreamed of
Emerging in the present,
Different and better
Than what we expected.

Birds have a sense
Of space and integral timing.
Aspects of life, side by side,
Caught in an instant, aligning.

Poetry serves no apparent purpose, yet we need it, like humanity.
So we can examine what we see, beauty, pain, everything in between.

In a concrete moment
Of encounter
Souls universalize the self.
What's there's true everywhere else.

PHOTO BY ANNIKA GOODMAN

Chrysalis Contemplation

Following the heat, gives you experience.
Unearned grace, deep desire trumps worthiness.
When we see, what could destroy, could enlighten us.
When we feel that glow on our face.

Picture you're in a chrysalis,
A quiet dark space of metamorphosis.
You linger in silence,
Embracing that threshold of change.

You rest as long as you can,
Relishing being in limbo.
Then there's a sliver of light,
The wonder of first flight.

When going into the full depths,
Or death, of anything,
We come out the other side,
Transformed, more alive.

On the other side, we're more forgiving of ourselves and others.
We know we've been led there, by a force larger than us.
We're more open, not holding on,
Accepting the gentle vortex, of that internal chrysalis.

Spiritual journeys proceed
Greater rings of inclusion.
And what's right in front of you,
Protects from self-delusion.

PAINTING BY LEAH SALOW

Portrait of an Ending

Do you see a house collapsed,
Taken over by woods.
Or remnants of an old church,
Concerts where an alter stood.

Endings are things we make, an artificial device,
Satisfying, convenient, a point's been made.
But stories march on, in step with time.
The ripple effect remains. The ripple effect remains.

You see a boardwalk
Extending into the sound,
Surrounded by riparian forest,
Changing tides, sea lions found.

Who else will take this path,
Embrace the slats, call it shelter?
Lives can be built on abstract patterns,
Woven, dangling helter skelter.

Endings not ending bring necessary uncertainty,
Give and take, eternal discovery.
The more we think we understand,
The more we see, nothing's bound by our plans.

Stories don't end but spin,
Away from one another,
Each one on its own course,
At times merging and asunder.

PHOTO BY ANNIKA GOODMAN

Carry One of You ～〜〇

An instrument can lead your play,
A different touch, quickening your response.
With a long-lost sense of well-being,
Waiting to see how it all shakes out.

It's small and can knock you out,
Words slid into a ventricle of the heart.
Your own opera house of melodrama,
You play your part, hope it's not just karma.

Death has a lot to teach us about living,
Hitting the bottom, where we're not in control.
There can be many deaths in our lives,
Tipping points, where we find our own souls.

The sorrowful can transform us,
Though it might destroy us too.
Resurrection's something rare and revolutionary,
Filled with promise, not hostility.

There's a path that begins, by realizing we've been loved all along.
It's a gift and a way of living,
Experienced in micro-sized rhythms,
Flowing through physically, like a song.

Loss makes you consider how grief works,
See your relationships differently,
Carry pieces of people with you,
Even while they're still here, and may carry one of you.

PAINTING BY ANDREW BOTTI

Beyond Ordinary Patterns   5/21-22/2022

You see gold melting on water,
An evanescent staircase.
You step on light, as it slowly winds down.

You surrender to the world of sound,
Mist of exhalation.
Ascending freely through the dark, floating in space.

Can't stop poetry. It's beyond ordinary patterns,
Addressing mystery and reality.
Sufficiently oblique, so we can tell the truth.
Not just the here and now, what we hope and see.

The experience of being yourself,
And the absent, mirroring other.
You channel the world. And reveal who you are.

Without humility and honesty,
It's really hard to move.
Those humble are naturally honest, about their own truth.

Like waxing and waning, the carousel swings up and down.
We learn not to quarrel gratuitously, what goes around comes around.

They're words to describe what's miraculous,
More like gestures than definition.
They point in a certain direction, like grace rather than instruction.

PHOTO BY ANNIKA GOODMAN

Join the Revelry

Rapport with the natural world, reflecting it back.
A child's artless sense of kinship, a certain restlessness.
There's a constant evolution,
With forms and going beyond constraints.

Love's a reciprocal dance.
Sometimes, to step forward, the other must step away,
Withdrawing for a moment,
The purpose to pull us back, towards them, away from the fray.

Babies have a sliding present, no past.
Living from emotion to emotion, opening up.
With children, there's a whole life,
Youth to get lost in and focus on.

We have a choice every day, to join the revelry.
There's nothing to prove, no fancy jewelry.
Nothing to protect if there's already respect.
If we're honest enough, we're more than enough. Everything changes.
Everything belongs.

When children tell a story,
We enter their invented world,
Letting go of our own.

PHOTO BY KATRINA WINZELER

Measure in a Second ⌇⌒⌒

A picture can give you a sense
That you're looking at nature,
But also looked upon by it,
Deliberating your stature.

Being there you become part of it,
Without being noticed,
Invisible so you can capture images,
The subject not looking in your eyes.

A collage can exist in a single frame.
Ones that look easy suggest beauty is common,
Help our fear that life is chaos,
A measure of a lifetime in a second.

A landscape may be changed,
With a variety of properties,
But the wind doesn't look at us,
An animal does.

Photographs give form to your
Understanding of what's in front of you,
The gaze of an animal, hinged on your position,
Evoking an archetype through an instance.

Photos memorialize
Not only the light in the instance,
But its effect,
And all that's affected.

V. A WARM EMBRACE

There's joy in the tentative new freedom to mingle with others. Something to embrace with gratitude. Hopefully, we can keep it, holding it gently, so it won't dissolve in our warm arms.

21. Memories Converge
22. Birds in Motion
23. Remembering to Play
24. Ocean's Optimism
25. Shapes in Silence
26. Contingency
27. Hard Reset
28. By Letter
29. World's Play
30. Presence Unadorned

PHOTO BY ANNIKA GOODMAN

SUMMER OF 1990 IN SALZBURG, AUSTRIA, WITH MY GREAT UNCLE SEPP'S GUITAR.
MEMORIES FROM THE PAST CAN LEAD TO INSIGHTS FOR THE PRESENT.
THIS SONG IS ABOUT THE SUMMER OF 1990 I SPENT IN AUSTRIA WHERE
MY FATHER IS FROM.

Memories Converge ‿⌒〇

When I was 19, in my father's country,
Spoke a different language, for that time.
Isn't it amazing how we can adapt, so easily to different circumstances,
Playing another part, that we hadn't imagined?

I busked in public gardens, got to know my relatives,
Entered historical sites, of significance,
Met a college friend, and took a trip to Budapest,
Hoping that summer, would never end.

To awaken is not about staying in the same place,
Just viewing a new vista from there.
It's to find a new sight,
Looking back with a new set of eyes. New eyes.

I found some old lyrics and scribbled out chords from then.
Rearranged and built on them.
Isn't it funny how perspectives can change, while some things still stay
the same,
How things when found, have meanings retained?

Looking at the world, through past eyes, I love the reinvention.
Getting inside a song, it's about transformation – hindsight, insight,
and maybe foresight.

A gal looks out from a picture, with her great uncle's guitar,
Wearing those Edelweiss earrings.
Isn't it startling how memories can collide, bring back thoughts and
people
in a surge,
Everything that rises, must converge.

PHOTO BY KATRINA WINZELER

Birds in Motion ✺

Birds not in flight, just conversing.
Something that makes me feel, serenity.
Not side by side, but in community.
Framed by branches, in this sanctuary.

It's their inner sense I see, entering one another's joy.
Hit with the glint of love, ordinary things change color.
Rooted in deeper knowledge, of what's true and beautiful.
Beyond dualistic judgments, of good, bad and meaningful.
It's their inner sense I see.

They're radical interaction, not perfection,
Living in friendship, not supremacy.
Balletic in motion, and agreed,
Holding any tension of controversy.

Inner peace doesn't hinge upon expectations or routines.
It's something not seen.
How precious that heartbeat and breath can be,
To lean with others, without a hierarchy.

When living things are caught in motion,
Obscuring particular qualities,
Images elevate to abstraction with empathy,
Blurred, yet with more mental acuity.

PHOTO BY ANNIKA GOODMAN

Remembering to Play

Some are born rememberers,
Holding together all the gaps,
Owning mistakes, forgiving failures,
Loving us into a deeper life, that loves us back.

It's the breath that warms and renews,
The spring that wells up in the eyes.
Beyond the momentary shadows,
The disguise of things we hide. Things we hide.

They want to serve others,
Instead of being served themselves,
Forgive life itself for not being everything,
Forgive others and themselves for not being perfect.

Watching a playground,
You see the interactions,
They don't need to be verbal,
For togetherness and satisfaction.

Play is a way to communicate, join a child on their own terms.
Playing's how children make the world their own.
Playing renews. We should remember to play too.

Some say there's a third eye of seeing,
Knowing something by being calmly present,
Viewing with the heart, what may not be visible,
Yet, truly essential.

PAINTING BY LEAH SALOW

Ocean's Optimism ⟿

6/21-23/2022

Mystics of the here and now, in limitations of mortality.
Gifts lived out and expanding, as we devote ourselves to that agency.
Like the waves that surround and shape, we know there are forces that
we can't escape.
Unlike rocks moved to change by the sea, we know aligning with the
water's the way to be.

We learn how to make art by refracting and rearranging,
The emotional atmosphere we live in.
Sometimes the deepest feelings, show themselves in restraint.
Sometimes the bigger picture, rises above our pain.

How do we make the best of both life and death,
If we never fully say goodbye?
For those we've loved, we need to be able to see beyond,
Being caught by a clash of the senses.

Presence is being awake, in our experience,
Detaching from inner stories.
Practicing when it's easy, so it will be there when it's onerous.
Muscle memory forces us to see.

Simplicity's about choice, choosing less rather than more,
Time for people, rather than possessions to store.
Living life lightly, delighting in the subtle and plain,
Song, dance, music and grace.

A moving ocean's optimism,
Opens us with its embrace.
A relaxed grasp with humor,
Frees us within, frees others to stay.

PHOTO BY ANNIKA GOODMAN

Shapes in Silence ∿

Silence, has a life of its own,
A being unto itself, foundation of reality,
Sympathetic resonance, with what's right in front of you,
Being awake in its presence.

When you look at a boundless horizon,
No animals or sounds,
Other than the friction of leaves, sand and motion.
Faced with yourself, thoughts abound.

Documentary and therapy, are the same coin.
What's the actual story? What's your view?
You can't hide behind, jargon or theory,
Just have to speak and show your truth.

A dualistic mind reads reality in simple binaries,
Thinks itself clever for picking a side,
Missing the real palette and authentic nuance,
In saying what you mean from the inside.

There's an elegance in the slopes and forms,
Mottled pattern across the landscape.
Constantly changing, particle by particle,
Always perfect, though a different shape.

PHOTO BY KATRINA WINZELER

Contingency ⤳

6/26/2022 Originally 2005
by Katrina Winzeler

I didn't ask for this. You didn't ask for your existence.
Visible and then, why do we feel loss of it.
Sometimes I try to fill it. Sometimes I strip it off in vain.
Visible less and then, why do we read in English?
Sometimes I like the darkness. Sometimes it creeps me out.
Oh what do ya do when there's no white bar back upon it.
And everything you depended on is gone.

I don't understand. I don't understand.
You're content to see me there. Kin pulls its mien.
Where the sky goes dark and, no one's at hand.
I scream, I don't understand, just don't understand.

I made my life. What a horrible thing.
Set freeze there, so that now I should rival me.
Where are we walking? Where do, we come from?
I know my hobo mass, but the explanation pulls a fast one.
We know how everything works. We know that meaning's fake.
When the earth meets her feet again, you wonder how much more you
can take.
Time is ticking … hon' it's getting late.

Love instability. Love what, you can't see.
These are the things, that'll save us all someday.
It's not a bad, price to pay.

PHOTO BY ANNIKA GOODMAN

Hard Reset 〜⌒ゝ

Who can say? Maybe some connections are too significant,
To be confined to one lifetime.
Or maybe we just need a lot of lives,
To learn what we need to learn.
When it's too dark to see color,
You know that with the darkness, you can still see.

Soul mates can make appearances
In our lives to fulfill roles.
Sometimes it leads to lessons,
But they can't stay, they have to go.

Souls like trees, can appear as subtraction,
Black voids in a less black sky.
We can paint them with a flashlight,
Lit for a second, up high.

The idea that what we deeply desire, may only be later revealed,
That it's something we must wait for, is not easy to accept.
Relinquishing control is a hard reset … hard reset ….

Soul mates can find us again eventually,
For another karmic issue,
Or maybe something from a past life,
Bleeds into the present, something new … something new ….

PAINTING BY ANDREA BOTTI

By Letter

To learn technique, is so you can help yourself,
When there's no one around.
A bag of tools, to be diagnostic,
Further your sound.

When culture changes, you've got to listen.
It can only make things better,
When we're not so attached, to the systems around us.
You can adjust things better, letter by letter.

Are purple mountains, majesty,
Or is that just in our heads?
Do they come back, in a vision
Or as part of a nightmare, instead?

To admit something's crumbling,
Is necessary for anything new.
By staying defiantly,
We resolve, to see it through.

Rigor can help, to get through discomfort,
'Cause feelings are not easy to unpack.
They are strong, legitimate and valid,
To explore yet keep intact.

PHOTO BY ANNIKA GOODMAN

World's Play 〜

Geisha friends in a past life,
Geisha meaning artist.
Sisters in a tea house,
Artists to the core.

See performers as alter egos,
Longing to wield their styles.
Maintain an alternate consciousness,
Behavior has a different emphasis.

Faith is finding ourselves, and what we desire,
New ways to begin each day.
Believing in and knowing, your own voice,
Adding to the remarkable chorus, of the world's play.

No lonely hearts, aching in a corner,
Suffering the tempests of life.
Helping people to see who they are,
And what they want to realize.

We can envision our work as drops in an ocean we are in,
With love and compassion downstream.
We are driven towards higher levels of inclusion,
Even if some go kicking and screaming.

The best criticism of the bad,
Is the practice of the better.
Opposite energy makes more of the same,
So we're acting to never say never.

SCULPTURES BY ERIC KAIN HUMPHREYS

Presence in absence, can be haunting but hopeful,
Like we're not alone.
Even when things are falling apart,
And no one else is home.

Presence can be interior images
Of social remembrance.
The question of forgetting
Another form of remembering.

What are those cerebral statues
That exist in our minds,
Stories told and reinvented?
Maybe fanciful, but in our lives.

It's not just about what happened,
But what people thought or imagined,
Even what they said did not occur,
Yet were invested in.

Wooden heads and hearts,
Cultural tradition in many forms,
What they hold inside for us,
Can be beautiful and unadorned

ACKNOWLEDGEMENTS

Many thanks to Andrew Botti, Eric Kain Humphreys, Katrina Winzeler, Leah Salow, Kira Seamon, Chuck Sheehan, my Dad, Dr. Werner Schroffner, my kids, Annika, Ari and Jake, and my husband, Josh, for your artistic contributions. These songs, whether posted for listening or in this book, would not be what they are without your inspiration and works. I am also grateful to my family for putting up with me and participating in as well as fostering creativity.

About the Author

Chiemi was born in Hawaii and lives with her family in Massachusetts. You can follow and access recordings of her songs at https://www.instagram.com/ingrid_chiemi/, https://www.facebook.com/ChiemisanMusic, https://soundcloud.com/user-377401109, https://chiemi1.bandcamp.com/,and https://www.youtube.com/channel/ UCzSMSHCECeHrw-Pmymg27LA.

For more information about Chiemi, go to www.ChiemiMusic.com.

Please also consider leaving a review on Amazon or Goodreads!

PHOTO BY ARI GOODMAN